US ARMY AIR ASSAULT & GENERAL SUPPORT HELICOPTER UNIT PATCHES
VOL 1: ACTIVE DUTY UNITS (2001-2021)

CW4 DAN McCLINTON (USA/RET)

OTHER BOOKS BY THE AUTHOR

MILITARY INSIGNIA

US ARMY AIR CAVALRY PATCHES (2001-2021)
US ARMY ATTACK HELICOPTER UNIT PATCHES (2001-2021)

PHOTOGRAPHY

37 MONTHS: IMAGES FROM THREE COMBAT TOURS IN IRAQ

MILITARY HISTORY

CRAZYHORSE: FLYING APACHE ATTACK HELICOPTERS WITH THE 1ST CAVALRY DIVISION IN IRAQ (2006-2007)

TABLE of CONTENTS

INTRODUCTION	page 4
1ST AIR CAVALRY BRIGADE	5
1ST COMBAT AVIATION BRIGADE	21
2ND COMBAT AVIATION BRIGADE	34
3RD COMBAT AVIATION BRIGADE	39
4TH COMBAT AVIATION BRIGADE	49
10TH COMBAT AVIATION BRIGADE	59
12TH COMBAT AVIATION BRIGADE	71
16TH COMBAT AVIATION BRIGADE	84
25TH COMBAT AVIATION BRIGADE	92
82ND COMBAT AVIATION BRIGADE	101
101ST COMBAT AVIATION BRIGADE	110
501ST COMBAT AVIATION BRIGADE	132
MISCELLANEOUS UNITS	141
CONTRIBUTORS	146

INTRODUCTION

Welcome to the 3rd in my series of books that feature the patches and insignia that were used by US Army Aviation Units from the 11th of September 2001 until 2021. While the first two books featured patches of the Air Cavalry and Attack helicopter units, this volume will focus on Assault and General Support aviation units or what some folks refer to as Lift units. I have attempted to make this book as complete as I possibly can. Given the nature of Army aviation and how patches are acquired and distributed, there is no way I will ever find EVERY patch that has ever been used. If when looking through this book you, the reader find that you have a patch that was not included I would request that you send and image of it and a short explanation to the email address that is at the end of this book so it might be included in future updates.

ORGANIZATION of this BOOK
While this subject has been discussed in the previous 2 volumes, it is worth noting again that 2001 found the US Army not just beginning to engage in a global conflict that would end up lasting over 20 years, but also starting a process that led to the renaming and moving of units across the force. In this volume units have been placed with either the parent unit they now operate with or with the last unit they were assigned to before being placed on the inactive roles.

MEDEVAC UNITS
Prior to around 2005 Medical Evacuation units (aka MEDEVAC) were owned by the Medical Service Corps and fell under the command of Medical Battalions which were outside the control of Combat Aviation Brigades and Army Aviation in general. Around 2005 these units began to be absorbed into the standard Army aviation structure. For example, the MEDEVAC company that was the 571st Medical Evacuation Company became C Company 2-227 AVN. Tracking down what all these units were designated as before their merger with traditional Army Aviation units is a rabbit-hole I chose not to go down. MEDEVAC and DUSTOFF have a proud history and frankly deserve a book of their own that includes their patches and insignia. If your unit patch isn't in this book, I apologize and beg your forgiveness, but frankly I had to draw the line somewhere.

KOREA
The designation of assignment of US Army Aviation units stationed in Korea is something that is bit of a challenge. Around the time of the big reorganization units that ended up elsewhere like 1-52 AVN operated in Korea assigned to either 8th Army or the 2nd Infantry Division. Much like the previously discussed MEDEVAC units, I had to draw a line somewhere, so I made the command decision to just cover units with the 2nd Aviation Regiment moniker like 2nd Battalion 2nd Aviation Regiment. Once again if I left your unit out, I apologize.

101st AIR ASSAULT DIVISION
Established as the Aviation Brigade 101st Airborne Division in 1986, the unit had 9 separate battalions under its control making it the largest aviation brigade in the United States Army. In 1997 the brigade split into 2 entities, the 101st Aviation Brigade and the 159th Aviation Brigade making the 101st the only division in the Army to have 2 aviation brigades. In 2015 the 159th Aviation Brigade was deactivated, which left the 101st Combat Aviation Brigade as the sole aviation brigade in the 101st. For the purposes of this book all the aviation units in the 101st have been listed under the 101st CAB. Any 159th CAB specific patches have been listed in their own section.

160th SOAR
Anyone that collects Army Aviation patches know that there are more than a few examples of patches that represent the 160th Special Operations Aviation Regiment. I have made the decision not to include those patches in this book. I served in the Army as an aviator for a little over 24 years and worked in and around the 160th SOAR several times. At no time did I ever see them wearing any of the patches that I have seen available on the INTERNET and other places. That doesn't invalidate those patches, but it does make it easier to make the decision to not include them in this book. For those that were hoping to see patches from the 160th, sorry maybe next time.

Now with all of that out of the way, I hope you enjoy this book. As always, all mistakes, typos and misidentification are solely my fault. All the goodness that you are about to see is because of the many people who were kind enough to share images of their collections, all credit goes to them. AIR ASSAULT!

1st Air Cavalry Brigade (1st ACB)

1st Cavalry Division, Fort Hood, Texas

HHC 1st ACB "WARLORDS"

F Company 227th AVN "NOMADS"

History of the 1st Air Cavalry Brigade (1st ACB)

The 1st Air Cavalry Brigade was constituted in the Regular Army as Headquarters and Headquarters Troop, Cavalry Brigade, 1st Cavalry Division at Fort Hood, Texas on 1 September 1984 and activated on 16 September 1984. The speed, mobility, and flexibility of the brigade provides the Division Commander with the organic capability to shape the entire battlefield and respond with the necessary tempo and lethality of modern warfare. The brigade is composed of the Headquarters and Headquarters Company, one attack battalion, one reconnaissance squadron, a general support aviation battalion, an air assault battalion, and an aviation support battalion.

The 1st Air Cavalry Brigade's mission is to find, fix, and destroy enemy forces using maneuver to concentrate and sustain combat power as an integrated member of a combined armed team. 1ACB destroys enemy forces using fire, maneuver, and shock effect. It conducts reconnaissance security operations and provides C2 support. As a member of the "First Team", the 1st Air Cavalry Brigade enhances the overall effectiveness of the division and gives the Division Commander a highly flexible, responsive, and lethal combat multiplier.

The 1ACB traces its history back to early 1963, when the Army began to gather helicopters into the 11th Air Assault Division and first tested the airmobile concept. After validation of the airmobile concept, the units were reassigned to the 1st Cavalry Division (Airmobile). On 1 August 1965, the 1st Cavalry Division was sent to Vietnam. 1st Cavalry Division Aviators participated in 14 campaigns and received seven unit decorations to include the Presidential Unit Citation (2 awards), the Valorous Unit Award (3 awards), the Meritorious Unit Commendation, the Republic of Vietnam Cross of Gallantry with Palm (3 awards), and the Republic of Vietnam Civil Action Honor Medal, First Class, during its 7 years of duty in Vietnam. The first Army Aviator to be awarded the Medal of Honor in the Vietnam War was a member of the 227th Aviation Battalion.

In late 1990, the brigade deployed to Saudi Arabia, where the unit prepared for combat in Operation Desert Shield. On 25 February 1991, with the onset of Operation Desert Storm, the brigade conducted a raid as part of the 1st Cavalry Division's deception plan against Iraqi forces. Later, the brigade served as the vanguard of the division's movement north to cut off a retreating Iraqi Republican Guard Division at Basra. The brigade received the Meritorious Unit Commendation for Southwest Asia.

The brigade again proved its timely responsiveness in January 1993, deploying command and control aircraft to Kuwait. With 48 hours notice, the brigade deployed to Somalia, where it flew over 500 hours of combat missions. On 16 October 1996, the brigade was reorganized and redesignated as Headquarters and Headquarters Company, Aviation Brigade, 1st Cavalry Division. The changing threat was next met in Bosnia, when in 1999, the brigade deployed to Operation Joint Forge. Units flew in the Balkans in support of Stabilization Force 4. Missions performed ranged from multi-national general support airborne command and control, to air movement operations. In recognition of their performance in the Balkans, 2nd Battalion, 227th Aviation Regimen was selected as the Army Aviation Association of America's (AAAA) Aviation Unit of the Year.

With the onset of Operation Iraqi Freedom in March 2003, the brigade deployed the 1st Battalion, 227th Aviation to Iraq to exercise their Longbow apaches in combat operations for the first time. There, they set conditions for the defeat of Saddam's Army and the liberation of Baghdad. In the early hours of 24 March 2003, Apache Longbows of the 1st Cavalry Division fought a fierce battle with units of Iraq's Republican Guard between the cities of Karbala and Al Hilah, south of Baghdad.

During March 2004, the brigade deployed to Operation Iraqi Freedom II as part of Task force Baghdad. The brigade developed and implemented new techniques for air/ground integration using lethal and agile teams, and was instrumental in enabling the first free elections in Iraq in 50 years. The brigade flew over 70,000 hours and was recognized with 84 awards for valor including a Silver Star and seven Distinguished Flying Crosses. During this deployment, the brigade was also recognized as the 2004 AAAA Aviation Unit of the Year.

History of 1st ACB continued...

The 1st air Cavalry Brigade deployed to Iraq in 2006 and conducted full spectrum combat operations in support of the "Surge" from Camp Taji, flying over 90,000 combat hours during eh 15 month deployment. During this deployment an Army Aviator from 1-227th Aviation was awarded the Distinguished Service Cross posthumously, the highest award for valor received by a First Team Trooper in Iraq. Upon redeployment in January 2008, the brigade reset and was fielded the CH-47F in preparation for its next deployment to Camp Taji in support of Operation Iraqi Freedom 09-10. The brigade witnessed the transformation of security responsibility to the Iraqi security apparatus and supported the Iraqi government as it accepted responsibility for ht safety and welfare of its people.

Following a fourth combat deployment to Iraq, the brigade deployed to Afghanistan in 2011, where it supported NATO and coalition forces in four of Afghanistan's six regional commands with multifunctional battalion task forces operating in 12 locations. Flying over 60,000 hours in some of the most demanding terrain, the brigade provided a full spectrum of aviation capabilities to US, ISAF, and Afghan security forces for 12 intense months.

The agile and lethal 1st Air Cavalry Brigade continues to "live the Legend" in the 1st Cavalry Division, as they have done since 1984. The 1st Air Cavalry Brigade stands ready to fight and win anytime and anywhere.

Information regarding deployments post 2011 were not available to the author at time of publication. Air Cavalry Brigade history courtesy of the 1st Cavalry Divsion Association (https://1cda.org/history/history-1acb/)

2nd Battalion 227th Aviation Regiment "LOBOS"

General Support Aviation Battalion, 1st Cavalry Division, FT Hood, TX

Battalion and Task Force patches

A Company 2-227 AVN "WEREWOLVES" / "VULTURES"

A Company continued...

B Company 2-227 AVN "VULTURES" / "BLACK CATS"

B Company continued...

C Company 2-227 AVN "GHOSTRIDERS" / "WITCHDOCTORS"

C Company continued...

  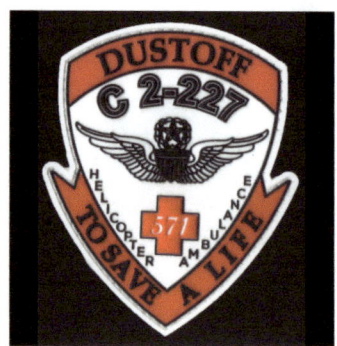  

  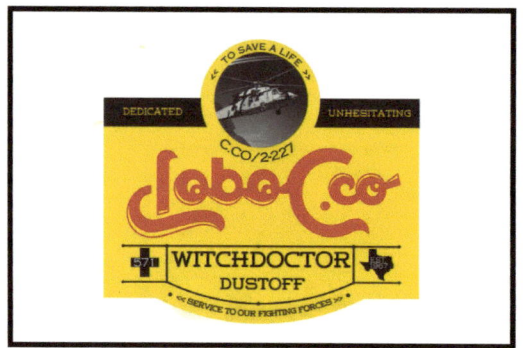

D Company 2-227 AVN "OUTLAWS"

E Company 2-227 AVN "RENEGADES"

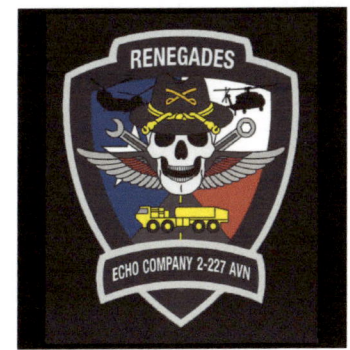

F Company 2-227AVN "RAVENS"

3rd Battalion 227th Aviation Regiment "SPEARHEAD"

Assault Helicopter Battalion, 1st Cavalry Division, FT Hood, TX

Battalion and Task Force patches

A Company 3-227 AVN "WEREWOLVES"

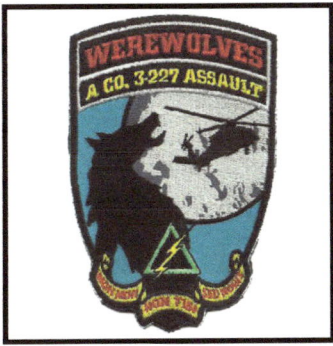 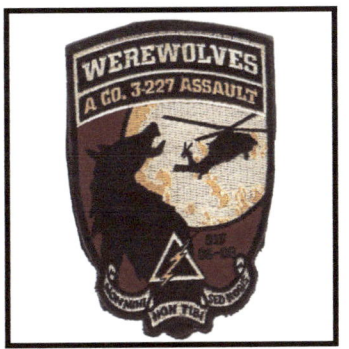   

B Company 3-227 AVN "JOKERS"

B Company continued...

C Company 3-227 AVN "GHOSTRIDERS"

C Company continued...

D Company 3-227 AVN "ROUGHNECKS"

E Company 3-227 AVN "REGULATORS"

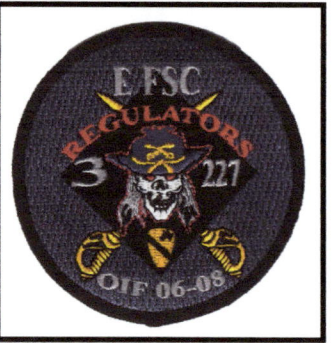

HHC 3-227 AVN

615th Aviation Support Battalion

2-227 & 3-227 AVN "OPERATION HURRICANE BOOGALOO"

Vulture Culture

Tracking the evolution of one unit's patch

Those that have more than a passing knowledge of how patches are designed and approved for Army Aviation units already know that it is quite rare for the patch for one aviation company to be essentially unchanged for years, much less decades. But, in the case of the Vultures of Alpha Company 2nd Battalion 227th Aviation Regiment that is exactly what has occurred.

Since the Vietnam War the design which was originated by the 162nd Aviation Company (Air Assault) has continued to today with it's basic elements intact. The Vulture and motto "STS" which stands for "Slicker Than Shit" have been on every patch from then until now, through numerous name changes and hundreds of commanders it has remained a constant. One look at the contents of this book will tell you what a rare occurrence this is. That is not to say that changes haven't been made because they obviously have. The appearance of the Vulture has changed several times, and many different things have appeared in the background over the years from American flags to Black Hawk helicopters. But overall they have been nothing if not consistent and in a world of constant change, that is one thing that should be celebrated.

(ABOVE L-R) The 162nd Aviation Company Patch from the Vietnam era. 2 patches from E Company 227th AVN 1st Cavalry Division. The company was still flying UH-1s at that time. A name and an aircraft change as the unit became B Company 4-227 and was assigned UH-60 Black Hawks. This was followed by another name change to B Company 2-227 AVN.

(BELOW L-R) The unit added a green square with lightning bolt to represent the markings that were seen on the doors of B Company 227 AVN aircraft in Vletnam. A final name change (for now) to A Compnay 2-227 AVN and some artwork changes with the current design seen on the far right.

1st Combat Aviation Brigade (1st CAB)//

1st Infantry Division, Fort Riley, Kansas

History of the 1st Combat Aviation Brigade (1st CAB)

The Combat Aviation Brigade, 1st Infantry Division, was originally formed from the assets of the Aviation Brigade, 1st Armored Division,[1] which had been created from the assets 1st Armored Division's 501st Aviation Battalion on 17 April 1986. Colonel James W. Lloyd, the first Aviation Brigade Commander, accepted the unit colors from Major General Dave R. Palmer, Commanding General, 1st Armored Division. (Note: Although often referred to as the "4th Brigade," the United States Army Center of Military History has confirmed that divisional aviation brigades are not numbered. The only exceptions are the 101st and 159th Aviation Brigades in the 101st Airborne Division (Air Assault), which has two aviation brigades.)

When formed, the Brigade consisted of the 10th and 501st Aviation Battalions, the 220th Aviation Company (Assault Helicopter), the 244th Aviation Company (Command Aviation) and the 61st Aviation Company (Maintenance). Brigade aircraft included 22 AH-1 Cobras, 38 OH-58s and 30 UH-1s.

On 16 November 1987 the 501st and 10th Aviation Battalions were reflagged as the 2nd and 3rd Battalions, 1st Aviation Regiment. Alpha Company, 501st became Golf and Hotel Companies under the 1st Armored Division and were designated again under the 3rd Infantry Division as 7th Battalion, 1st Aviation Regiment. The 61st Aviation Company (Maintenance) was reflagged as Company I, 1st Aviation Regiment.

In May 1988, the 1st Squadron, 1st Cavalry Regiment completed the conversion from a pure ground squadron to an air/ground squadron and moved from Schwabach to Katterbach. In late 1998, the 1st Squadron, 1st Cavalry turned in its M60A3s and received 40 M3 Cavalry Fighting Vehicles (CFV).

In July 1989, 2nd Battalion, 1st Aviation Regiment inactivated in Germany and the colors reactivated as an AH-64 Apache battalion at Fort Hood, Texas.

The "Strike Eagles" returned to Ansbach Army Heliport on 24 May 1990 becoming the first divisional AH-64 attack helicopter battalion stationed in Germany.

In November 1990, Company I, 1st Aviation was reflagged as the 9th Battalion, 1st Aviation Regiment. "Eagle Support" was designed to provide dedicated support to the aviation brigade. The unit later became 603rd Support Battalion (Aviation) under 3rd Infantry Division.

In December 1990, COL Daniel J. Petrosky led the brigade to Southwest Asia with the 1st Armored Division and conducted combat operations. For its accomplishments in Operation Desert Storm, the brigade was selected as AAAA unit of the year in 1991.

Shortly after the unit returned and in conjunction with the reorganization of USAREUR, the "Iron Eagle" Brigade joined the 3rd Infantry Division. The 1st Squadron, 1st Cavalry was inactivated and turned in its equipment. Its colors were transferred to the divisional cavalry squadron of the 1st Armored Division.

The Aviation Brigade was inactivated in January 1996 at Fort Riley, Kansas, and was reactivated as Aviation Brigade, 1st Infantry Division, in Katterbach, Germany on 15 February 1996, becoming an integral part of the Big Red One. The Aviation Brigade supported numerous contingency operations throughout Europe and Southwest Asia.

In 1997, the Aviation Brigade deployed to Bosnia and Herzegovina to provide aviation support for Operation Joint Forge. In 1999 the Aviation Brigade deployed to Kosovo as a part of the Multi-National Brigade East to provide aviation support to Operation Joint Endeavor. The Aviation Brigade continued operations in Kosovo through July 2003.

History of the 1st CAB continued...

In early 2003, the Aviation Brigade prepared for combat operations in support of Operation Iraqi Freedom. Elements of the Aviation Brigade deployed to Turkey to provide general aviation support to AFOR Turkey and the 1st Infantry Division. This support effort was made without aircraft as the battalion was stuck in Kosovo on "unofficial" deployment orders and after three months of trying to get to Iraq through Turkey the Division was turned around and the aviation elements relocated back to Katterbach.

Upon redeployment, the Aviation Brigade welcomed the 6th Squadron, 6th Cavalry Regiment "Six Shooters" to the brigade as part of its aviation transformation and, on 13 June 2005, inactivated the 1st Squadron, 1st Aviation Regiment "Gunfighters," the colors of which departed for the Longbow Unit Fires Training Program (UFTP).

The Aviation Brigade completed a fifteen month deployment to Iraq supporting Operation Iraqi Freedom 07-09. Conducting operations from forward operating base Speicher, the Aviation Brigade provided attack, assault, and general aviation support throughout central Iraq. During the deployment, the brigade flew over 20,000 combat flight hours providing aviation combat and combat support to the 1st Infantry Division. The unit's participation was critical during the OIF "surge". During this time, the CAB was led by Col Jesse Farrington and CSM Darrell "Buddy" Wallace.

In March 2010, the Combat Aviation Brigade deployed to Iraq for a 12-month rotation in support of Operation Iraqi Freedom, as well as to usher in and spearhead Operation New Dawn in September of the same year.

Along with its parent 1st Infantry Division, the Combat Aviation Brigade is currently assigned to Fort Riley, Kansas. The current configuration is as follows:

HHC, Combat Aviation Brigade
1st Battalion (Attack Reconnaissance), 1st Aviation Regiment
2nd Battalion (General Support), 1st Aviation Regiment
3rd Battalion (Assault), 1st Aviation Regiment
1st Squadron, 6th Cavalry Regiment
601st Aviation Support Battalion

2nd Battalion 1st Aviation Regiment "FIGHTING EAGLES"
General Support Aviation Battalion, 1st Infantry Division, FT Riley, KS

Battalion and Task Force patches

A Company 2-1 AVN "PHANTOMS" / "FLYING ACES"

B Company 2-1 AVN "KNIGHTHAWKS" / "DIESEL"

B Company continued...

C Company 2-1 AVN "NIGHT RAVEN" / "DUSTOFF"

C Company continued...

D Company 2-1 AVN "ROUGHNECKS"

E Company 2-1 AVN "ELIMINATORS"

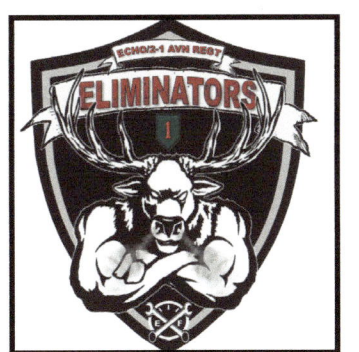

F Company 2-1 AVN "PHANTOMS"

HHC 2-1 AVN "HEADHUNTERS"

3rd Battalion 1st Aviation Regiment "NIGHTMARES"

Assault Helicopter Battalion, 1st Infantry Division, FT Riley, KS

Battalion and Task Force patches

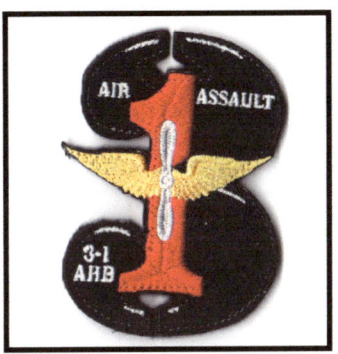
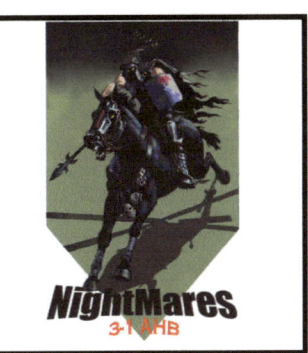

A Company 3-1 AVN "BLACK CATS"

B Company 3-1 AVN "BLACK KNIGHTS"

C Company 3-1 AVN "BLACK SHEEP"

D Company 3-1 AVN "DRAGON SLAYERS"

   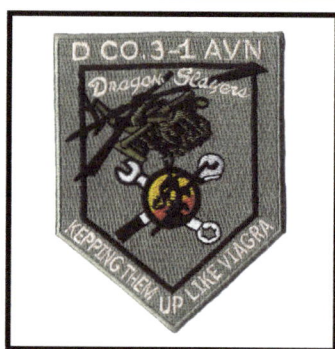

E Company 3-1 AVN "EXECUTIONERS"	601st Aviation Support Battalion

2nd Combat Aviation Brigade (2nd CAB) "TALON"

2nd Infantry Division, Camp Humphreys, Republic of Korea

AUTHOR'S NOTE: At the time of publication there was no comprehensive history of the 2nd Combat Aviation Brigade available to be included in this book. The 2nd CAB has been assigned to the 2nd Infantry Division and stationed in Korea during its entire existence and while elements of this CAB have deployed to combat during the GWOT, the BDE itself has not been asked to leave the Korean peninsula.

2nd Battalion 2nd Aviation Regiment "WILD CARDS"
Assault Helicopter Battalion, 2nd Infantry Division, Republic of Korea

Battalion patches

A Company 2-2 AVN "MUSTANGS"

    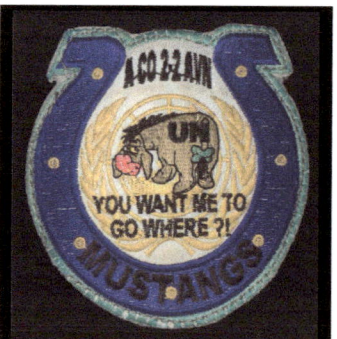

B Company 2-2 AVN "RENEGADES"

B Company continued...

C Company 2-2 AVN "COMANCHES"

3rd Battalion 2nd Aviation Regiment "NIGHTMARE"
General Support Aviation Battalion, 2nd Infantry Division, Republic of Korea

Battalion patches

A Company 3-2 AVN "DRAGONS"

B Company 3-2 AVN "INNKEEPERS"

C Company 3-2 AVN "DMZ DUSTOFF"

| C Company continued... | D Company 3-2 AVN "ACES HIGH" |

| E Company 3-2 AVN "ENFORCERS" | F Company 3-2 AVN "SKY MASTERS" |

| HHC 3-2 AVN "TRANSPORTERS" |

3rd Combat Aviation Brigade (3rd CAB) "MARNE AIR"

3rd Infantry Division, Hunter Army Airfield, Georgia

E Company 3rd AVN "CHAOS"	HHC 3rd CAB

History of the 3rd Combat Aviation Brigade (3rd CAB)

Originally designated the 3rd Aviation Company, the 3rd Combat Aviation Brigade was activated and assigned to the 3rd Infantry Division on July 1, 1957 at Fort Benning, Georgia. Twenty-seven years later, on November 16, 1984, the CAB was provisionally activated as the U.S. Army's first combat aviation brigade in a mechanized infantry division. The brigade was officially activated March 15, 1985 and designated the 4th Brigade, 3rd Infantry Division and then inactivated on August 16, 1991. It was reactivated on February 16, 1996 at Fort Stewart, Georgia as part of the redesignation of the 24th Infantry Division (Mechanized) as the 3rd Infantry Division (Mechanized).

February 1998 the 3rd Combat Aviation Brigade deployed to Kuwait as part of the 3rd Infantry Division's mission in support of Operation Desert Thunder. At the time the brigade was organized to provide 3rd Infantry Division with a maneuver brigade consisting of an attack helicopter battalion, a general support aviation battalion, and a cavalry squadron.

From September 2000 to October 2001, elements of 3rd CAB deployed to Bosnia-Herzegovina for Stabilization Force (SFOR) 8 and SFOR 9 and enforcement of the Dayton Peace Accords. The Stabilization Force has a unified command and is NATO-led under the political direction and control of the Alliance's North Atlantic Council, as stipulated by the Peace Agreement.

Less than a year after 9/11, the 3rd CAB deployed to Kuwait in support of OIF. On March 20, 2003, the brigade's helicopters served as part of the 3rd Infantry Division's main effort on the March to Baghdad. During the battle at An Nasiriah, the brigade shaped the battlespace in order for 3rd Brigade Combat Team, 3rd Infantry Division to destroy enemy units near the Highway 1 Bridge and Tallil Airbase. After the fall of Baghdad, the brigade continued to play a vital role in the ongoing fight for the security of the city and the country.

In 2004, the unit was redesigned as the U.S. Army's first modular Combat Aviation Brigade. Soon thereafter, the brigade deployed to Iraq in January 2005 in support of Operation Iraqi Freedom III. The brigade significantly increased its ability to operate 24 hours a day for an indefinite period of time providing an unprecedented level of aviation combat power to the division. The brigade flew more than 80,000 hours in support of more than 26,000 combat missions.

In May 2007, as part of the "Surge," the 3rd CAB deployed to Iraq again, this time in support of Operation Iraqi Freedom V. During the Surge, the 3rd CAB was tasked with supporting the main mission of Multi-National Division-Center stopping the flow of accelerants into Baghdad. Over a 15 month deployment, the brigade completed more than 250 air assaults resulting in numerous arrests and captures of high value targets and other enemy fighters, and executed 5,700 MEDEVAC missions supporting Coalition Forces, Iraqi Army and local nationals. The brigade accounted for 64% of the Multi-National Division-Center enemy killed in action and more than 80 wounded in action. The brigade also moved over 205,000 personnel and 21 million pounds of cargo around the battlefield.

The 3rd CAB returned to Hunter Army Airfield in August of 2008, preparing for another deployment. Less than eight months after learning of the new mission in Afghanistan, the 3rd CAB, reorganized as Task Force Falcon, joined the surge into Afghanistan in November 2009. The arrival of the 3rd CAB marked a new chapter for the brigade and the 3rd Infantry Division as the Combat Aviation Brigade was the first brigade-sized element from the Marne Division to serve in OEF X. Task Force Falcon flew in excess of 160,000 combat flight hours and provided much needed humanitarian relief efforts to both Afghanistan and Pakistan.

History of the 3rd CAB continued...

On January 9, 2010, Task Force Falcon assumed responsibility of US Army conventional rotary wing aviation operations across Regional Commands – South, Southwest, and West supporting U.S. conventional and special operations forces, International Security Assistance Forces, and Afghan National Security Forces. The Falcon Team provided continuous attack, reconnaissance and security, medical evacuation, personnel and cargo transport, downed aircraft recovery, as well as deliberate and hasty air assault capabilities in support of ground forces. Task Force Falcon provided flexibility and freedom of maneuver to enable ground forces to extend their security operations and assist Afghan National Security forces with independent operations. Partnered missions proved essential in assisting Government of the Islamic Republic of Afghanistan to achieve its objective of providing independent security of the people of Afghanistan.

During Operation Enduring Freedom XIII, Task Force Falcon flew over 100,000 hours, averaging almost 12,000 hours per month during the height of the fighting season, and supported 625 deliberate operations, 2,000 MEDEVAC missions, and moved 4.9 million pounds of cargo and 15,000 personnel.

Task Force Falcon expanded the capabilities of previous units, while establishing their legacy through innovation and progress. MEDEVAC aircraft increased the use of critical blood transfusions during flight and added back wall medics and emergency critical care nurses to enable life saving operations. The task force completed the largest Forward Operating Base closure in Regional Command – South during OEF XIII – FOB Wolverine – ahead of schedule, while providing continued aviation support in Zabul Province. In April 2010, when a sudden hailstorm grounded 84 helicopters on Kandahar, the task force repaired all damaged aircraft within 3 weeks without a gap in air support to teammates on the ground, illustrating the unmatched dedication of Falcon maintainers.

While Task Force Falcon's tour was marked with successes and progress for Afghan Forces, it was not without great hardship associated with the loss of seven Falcon warriors. As we continue to hold our fallen heroes and their loved ones in our thoughts, we remain dedicated to the mission to honor their sacrifices. Each of our fallen died as they lived: brave and dedicated to family, duty, country, and the security of Afghanistan. They will never be forgotten.

3rd CAB History courtesy of the US Army (https://home.army.mil/stewart/index.php/units/3rdCAB)

2nd Battalion 3rd Aviation Regiment "KNIGHTHAWKS"
General Support Aviation Battalion, 3rd Infantry Division, Hunter AAF, GA

Battalion patches

A Company 2-3 AVN "STORM" / "BARNSTORMERS"

B Company 2-3 AVN "BARNSTORMERS" / "HERCULES"

| B Company continued... |

| C Company 2-3 AVN "MARNE DUSTOFF" |

| 2015-16 LLAMA Platoon Tab |

D Company 2-3 AVN "DRAGONS"	E Company 2-3 AVN "EAGLES"	F Company 2-3 AVN "PHOENIX"

4th Battalion 3rd Aviation Regiment "MARNE ASSAULT" / "BRAWLERS"

Assault Helicopter Battalion, 3rd Infantry Division, Hunter AAF, GA

Battalion and Task Force patches

FUN FACT: 4th Battalion, 3rd Aviation Regiment was originally constituted in the Regular Army on 23 April 1957 as the 3rd Aviation Company and assigned to the 3rd Infantry Division. Officially activated on 1 July 1957 at Fort Benning, Georgia, it was reorganized and redesignated twice before moving to the state of Franconia, Germany in June of 1964 as Headquarters and Headquarters Detachment, 3rd Aviation Battalion. Army demands for manpower and equipment in Vietnam contributed to the deactivation of the unit in 1967.

On 21 May 1972, the unit was reactivated and redesignated as the Aviation Company, 3rd Infantry Division based in the Wurzburg area of Franken. It was reorganized and redesignated as Headquarters and Headquarters Company, 3rd Aviation Battalion on 21 August 1978 and later occupied the newly built aviation facilities at Giebelstadt Army Airfield. During this tenure in Europe, the unit participated in numerous return of forces to Europe exercises, referred to as "REFORGER," and maintained patrols on the borders of east and west Germany. During REFORGER '77, the unit conducted the first airmobile operations in Europe.

The unit was redesignated as Company D, 3rd Aviation on 16 August 1987, relieved from assignment to the 3rd Infantry Division, and assigned to the 2nd Armored Division at Fort Hood, Texas. The unit was inactivated at Fort Hood, Texas on 15 March 1991.

To better support the nation's war on terrorism, the Chief of Staff of the Army ordered a review of Army organization for combat which resulted in significant organizational changes. To meet the requirements of aviation transformation, 9th Battalion, 101st Aviation Regiment was selected to reorganize under the Aviation Brigade of the 3rd Infantry Division. In May 2004, 9th Battalion, 101st Aviation Regiment was reflagged as 4th Battalion, 3rd Aviation Regiment (Assault) at Fort Campbell, Kentucky, and assigned to the Aviation Brigade of the 3rd Infantry Division, the first aviation unit of action formed under the army transformation plan.

A Company 4-3 AVN "SPIDERS"

B Company 4-3 AVN "BLACK HEARTS"

C Company 4-3 AVN "RAVENS"

D Company 4-3 AVN "DEMONS"

603rd Aviation Support Battalion

4th Combat Aviation Brigade (4th CAB) "IRON EAGLES"

4th Infantry Division, Fort Hood, Texas (2001-2011) / Fort Carson, Colorado (2013-2021)

History of the 4th Combat Aviation Brigade (4th CAB)

The "Ivy Eagles" were first activated as the 4th Aviation Company, 4th Infantry Division, at Fort Lewis, Washington, April 1, 1957. It was then reorganized and redesignated Oct. 1, 1963, as the Headquarters and Headquarters Company, 4th Aviation Battalion.

The 4th Aviation Battalion deployed to the Republic of Vietnam in September 1966, where it participated in multiple campaigns and was awarded two Republic of Vietnam Crosses of Gallantry and one Republic of Vietnam Civil Action Honor Medal. The unit redeployed to the U.S. in 1970 where it was inactivated at Fort Lewis, Washington, Dec. 4, 1970.

The 4th Aviation Battalion was activated at Fort Carson, Colorado, and redesignated the Aviation Company, 4th Inf. Div., Nov. 21, 1972. It was again reorganized and redesignated March 17, 1980, as HHC, 4th Aviation Battalion, and again Aug. 16, 1987, as 4th Aviation. In 1995, the unit relocated to Fort Hood, Texas, with the 4th Inf. Div. On Oct. 1, 2005, the unit was redesignated as the 4th Aviation Regiment.

The 4th Combat Aviation Brigade, 4th Inf. Div., deployed in 2005 and 2008 in support of Operation Iraqi Freedom and was awarded two Meritorious Unit Citations. The unit's most recent deployment was in 2010 in support of Operation Enduring Freedom, after which 4th CAB was awarded a Valorous Unit Award. Task Force Iron Eagle supported 22 allied nations across four Regional Commands, the largest geographical area of any combat aviation brigade.

The 4th CAB, 4th Inf. Div., was inactivated at Fort Hood, Texas, September 2011. The 4th CAB HHC was reactivated July 2, 2013, at Fort Carson, Colorado.

The 2nd General Support Aviation Battalion, 4th Avn. Reg., 4th CAB, was the first battalion to reactivate at Fort Carson, Colorado, in April 2013. In May 2014, the remaining four battalions that comprise the 4th CAB now were activated. They are the 6th Attack Reconnaissance Squadron, 17th Cavalry Regiment; 3rd Assault Helicopter Battalion, 4th Avn. Reg.; 4th Attack Reconnaissance Battalion, 4th Avn. Reg.; and 404th Aviation Support Battalion.

The 4th ARB deployed in May 2018 to the U.S. Central Command area of operations to support Operation Freedom's Sentinel (OFS), Operation Inherent Resolve (OIR) and Operation Spartan Shield (OSS).

The 4th CAB deployed in June 2018 to Europe to support the Atlantic Resolve mission, which builds readiness, increases interoperability and enhances the bonds between ally and partner militaries with multinational training events in Bulgaria, Estonia, Hungary, Latvia, Lithuania, Poland and Romania.

4th CAB History courtesy of the US Army (https://www.carson.army.mil/units/4ID.html)

2nd Battalion 4th Aviation Regiment "MUSTANGS"

General Support Aviation Battalion, 4th Infantry Division, FT Carson, CO

Battalion and Task Force patches

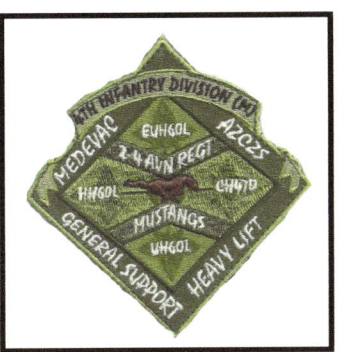

A Company 2-4 AVN "BANSHEES" / "KNIGHTHAWKS" / "BLACKJACKS"

B Company 2-4 AVN "BANSHEES" / "CLYDESDALES"

B Company continued...

C Company 2-4 AVN "COYOTES" / "LONESTAR DUSTOFF" / "ARCHANGEL DUSTOFF"

C Company continued...

  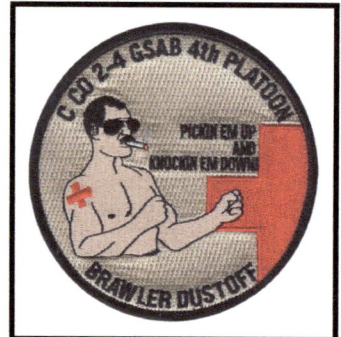 

D Company 2-4 AVN "MAVERICKS"

F Company 2-4 AVN

HHC 2-4 AVN "NIGHTHAWKS" / "OUTLAWS"

3rd Battalion 4th Aviation Regiment "COMANCHE"

Assualt Helicopter Battalion, 4th Infantry Division, FT Carson, CO

Battalion and Task Force patches

A Company 3-4 AVN "TOMAHAWKS"

  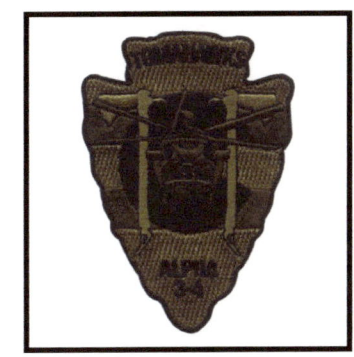  

B Company 3-4 AVN "BRAVES"

C Company 3-4 AVN "WARRIORS"

D Company 3-4 AVN "DARK RIDERS"

E Company 3-4 AVN "WARPATH"   404th Aviation Support Battalion "IRON EAGLE PROVIDERS"

10th Combat Aviation Brigade (10th CAB)

10th Mountain Division, Fort Drum, New York

D Company 10th AVN "VALKYRIE" / "SLAYER"	HHC 10th CAB "RENEGADES"	TASK FORCE CENTAUR OEF VII

History of the 10th Combat Aviation Brigade (10th CAB)

The 10th Aviation was constituted on Sept. 21, 1965, in the Regular Army as Headquarters and Headquarters Detachment, 10th Aviation Battalion. The unit activated on Aug. 23, 1965, at Fort Benning, Georgia, and it was redesignated as Headquarters and Headquarters Company, 10th Aviation Battalion, on Dec. 1, 1968.

The 10th Aviation was an important contributor to the U.S. Army's efforts in Vietnam. The unit provided critical aviation support in the first Tet counter-offensive, and it distinguished itself by successfully fulfilling this vital role. The 10th Aviation regularly repeated this standard for success in the intervening years and was recognized for valorous acts at Dak To and Tuy Hoa, receiving Commendations (Army) and five awards for gallantry from the Republic of South Vietnam. The 10th Aviation was inactivated Dec. 30, 1980, at Fort Lewis, Washington.

On July 2, 1988, the 10th Aviation Brigade was reactivated at Griffiss Air Force Base in Rome, New York, as part of the 10th Mountain Division (Light Infantry); it relocated to Fort Drum, New York, in 1990. Since then, it has played a key role in all division missions, to include support for Hurricane Andrew Relief in south Florida, Operations Restore Hope and Continue Hope in Somalia, Operation Uphold Democracy in Haiti, SFOR and KFOR missions in Bosnia and Kosovo, and most recently, Operations Iraqi Freedom in Iraq and Operation Enduring Freedom in Afghanistan. In each instance, the brigade demonstrated its capability to rapidly deploy and conduct aviation missions upon arrival while emphasizing safety and readiness.

In July 2003, the 10th Aviation Brigade Headquarters deployed to Bagram Airfield, and 2nd Battalion, 10th Aviation Regiment, deployed to Kandahar Airfield in support of Operation Enduring Freedom (OEF) IV. While deployed, 10th Aviation Brigade assumed command of Task Force Panther, Task Force Talon, and Task Force Red Dawg (U.S. Marine Corps), and the brigade was renamed Combined Joint Task Force Falcon.

In January 2006, the 10th Aviation Brigade Headquarters, along with the newly formed 3rd General Support Aviation Battalion, 10th Aviation Regiment, and 277th Aviation Support Battalion, deployed to Bagram, with 2-10 Aviation again deploying to Kandahar, this time with a slice of 277th ASB. Upon completion of their mission in support of OEF VII, the units returned to Fort Drum.

In October 2008, the 10th CAB Headquarters, along with 1-10 Aviation, 2-10 Aviation, 3-10 Aviation and 277th ASB, deployed to Contingency Operating Base Speicher, while 6th Squadron, 6th Cavalry Regiment, deployed to Mosul in support of Operation Iraqi Freedom VIII.

In October 2010, the 10th CAB Headquarters, along with Task Force Phoenix (3-10 Aviation), and Task Force Mountain Eagle (277th ASB) deployed to Bagram Airfield, while Task Force Knighthawk (2-10 Aviation) deployed to Forward Operating Base Shank, Task Force Tigershark (1-10 Aviation) deployed to Salerno, and Task Force Six Shooters (6-6 Cavalry) deployed to Jalalabad Airfield to support Operation Enduring Freedom XI.

In February 2012, the 10th CAB Headquarters, along with TF Phoenix (3-10 Aviation) deployed to Bagram Airfield, while TF Knighthawk (2-10 Aviation) deployed to FOB Shank, and TF Tigershark (1-10 Aviation) deployed to Salerno in support of Operation Enduring Freedom XIV.

History of the 10th CAB continued...

In February 2013, the brigade successfully deployed to Afghanistan in support of Operation Enduring Freedom.

In February 2015, D/10 "Gray Eagle" Company deployed to Afghanistan in support of Operation Freedom's Sentinel.

In October 2015, 6th Squadron, 6th Cavalry Regiment, deployed to South Korea with their OH-58D Kiowa helicopters. After their return from the rotation, the airframe was retired in July 2016, and 6-6 Cavalry transitioned into a heavy attack reconnaissance squadron (HARS) flying AH-64D Apache helicopters and RQ-7 Shadow unmanned aerial vehicles.

In March 2016, Soldiers of 1st Attack Reconnaissance Battalion, 10th Aviation Regiment, deployed to Iraq and Kuwait in an advisory role as part of Operation Inherent Resolve and Operation Spartan Shield.

In January 2017, D/10 "Gray Eagle" Company deployed to Iraq and Kuwait in support of both Operation Spartan Shield and Operation Inherent Resolve.

In February 2017, Soldiers of 10th CAB, augmented by 1-501st Attack Reconnaissance Battalion, 1st Combat Aviation Brigade, deployed across Europe in support of NATO and Atlantic Resolve 2.0.

In September 2017, 6-6 Cavalry returned to South Korea for a nine-month rotation to augment 2nd Combat Aviation Brigade, this time as an H-ARB.

Today, the 10th Combat Aviation Brigade stands ready to deploy in support of contingency operations worldwide.

10th CAB history courtesy of the US Army (https://home.army.mil/drum/index.php/units-tenants/10th-CAB)

2nd Battalion 10th Aviation Regiment "KNIGHTHAWK"

Assault Helicopter Battalion, 10th Mountain Division, FT Drum, NY

Battalion and Task Force patches

A Company 2-10 AVN "VOODOO STRIKE FORCE"

B Company 2-10 AVN "LYCANS" / "MOUNTAIN HAWKS"

C Company 2-10 AVN "WARLORDS"

   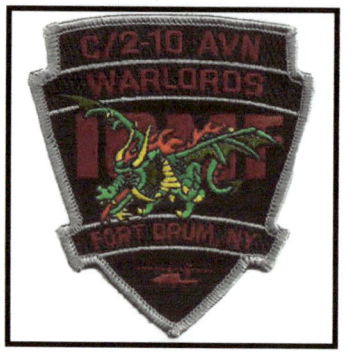 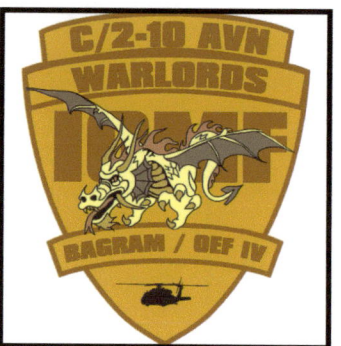

D Company 2-10 AVN "DRAGONHAWKS"

E Company 2-10 AVN "KNIGHT RIDERS" / "REGULATORS"

F Company 2-10 AVN "FIREHAWKS"

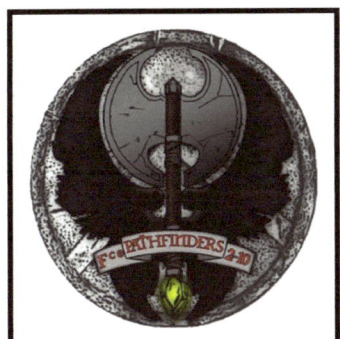 

F Troop 2-10 AVN "ACES"

G Company 2-10 AVN "INTRUDERS"

HHC 2-10 AVN "NOMADS"

3rd Battalion 10th Aviation Regiment "PHOENIX"
General Support Aviation Battalion, 10th Mountain Division, FT Drum, NY

Battalion and Task Force patches

A Company 3-10 AVN "WAR ANGELS"

B Company 3-10 AVN "MOUNTAIN MOVERS" / "COLOSSAL"

C Company 3-10 AVN "MOUNTAIN DUSTOFF"

 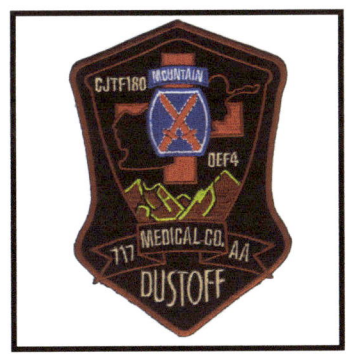   

1st Platoon (2020)

D Company 3-10 AVN "DAMAGE INC"

E Company 3-10 AVN "EXECUTIONERS"

F Company 3-10 AVN "FIREHAWKS"

HHC 3-10 AVN "HOOLIGANS"

12th Combat Aviation Brigade (12th CAB) "GRIFFIN"

Katterbach Army Airfield, Germany

HHC 12th CAB "WARRIORS"

12th CAB History since 9/11

Following the September 11th attacks in 2001, the 12th Aviation Brigade's first contributions to the war on terror were a joint effort with the U.S. Navy's Sixth Fleet in the Eastern Mediterranean Sea and in support of Operation Enduring Freedom. UH-60 Blackhawks from 3-158th Assault Helicopter Battalion participated in the fleet's Maritime Interdiction Operations, launching from the decks of U.S. Navy ships to conduct aerial surveillance of ships and to carry boarding parties during raids on suspect vessels. Also in support of Operation Enduring Freedom, Soldiers from 3-58 Aviation Regiment deployed to Afghanistan from 2002 to 2003 in order to perform the Air Traffic Control mission in the south of that country.

Starting in October 2002, the 12th Aviation Brigade deployed to Kuwait in anticipation of war with Iraq. With the addition of an Attack Battalion from 1st Cavalry Division, the 12th Aviation Brigade conducted patrols along the Kuwait-Iraq border until the beginning of the ground war in March. When the invasion began, these units were the first non-Special Operations helicopters to cross the border in Operation Iraqi Freedom. The brigade continued to operate in Iraq until early 2004.

In February 2005, the 12th Aviation Brigade deployed to Afghanistan as Task Force Griffin operating as two task-organized battalion task forces, Sabre and Storm, in the regional commands east and south. In November 2005, an Earthquake struck the Kashmiri region of Pakistan, causing nearly 75,000 deaths and injuring more than 100,000 people in Pakistan. Cut off from assistance by the damage, more than 120,000 people created a very complicated international relief effort. The 12th Aviation Brigade dispatched CH-47 Chinook helicopters to aid in the crisis, delivering much needed food and medical supplies, and transporting victims to safety from remote areas in the mountains of Pakistan.

In early 2006, V Corps consolidated units from the 11th Aviation Regiment and 12th Aviation Brigade. The 11th Aviation Regiment was inactivated. During the realignment process, the second Israeli-Lebanon war started, and the 12th Aviation Brigade again sent helicopters to Cyprus to support the evacuation of civilians from Lebanon in a second Beirut Air Bridge.

On August 6, 2006, the units of 4th Brigade, 1st Infantry Division combined with units of both the 12th Aviation Brigade and the former 11th Aviation Regiment were re-designated as the 12th Combat Aviation Brigade.

Following the transformation into the 12 CAB, the brigade continued to support the ongoing conflicts in Iraq and Afghanistan. The 12 CAB deployed for the first time as a named Combat Aviation Brigade to Iraq in July 2007. The headquarters operated from Balad as the Multi-National Corps-Iraq's Corps Aviation Brigade over a four-month period before relocating to Taji along with 3-158th Assault Helicopter Battalion (AHB) and a Forward Logistical Element (FLE) from the 412th Aviation Support Battalion (ASB). Additionally, the 2-159th Attack Reconnaissance Battalion (ARB) and 5-158th General Support Aviation Battalion (GSAB) went to work as the Aviation Brigade under Multi-National Division-Baghdad. The remainder of 412th, along with 2-159th ARB and 5-158th GSAB remained in Balad under the command of Task Force 49 from Alaska. During this period, 3-58 Aviation Regiment (Air Traffic Services) was reflagged 3-58 Airfield Operations Battalion (AOB). The Brigade returned to Germany after 15 months of combat in support of the surge operations in Iraq.

The 3-159th ARB deployed separately to Iraq in August 2008 attached to Task Force 34, operating out of Balad and Baghdad. The 3-159th conducted a hand-over with 2-159th and assumed the same mission as the 12 CAB redeployed. The 3-159th returned to Germany a year later, just in time for the rest of the Brigade to deploy to Iraq one last time.

12th CAB History continued...

In November 2009, while much of the CAB deployed to Iraq, 5-158th GSAB, and a company from 2-159th ARB, which deployed separately to Shindand Afghanistan, and 3-159th ARB and a majority of 1-214th GSAB remained in Germany. Most of 2-159th ARB was in Northern Iraq, while 3-158th AHB found its forces assigned to both Balad and to Baghdad. Some elements of 1-214th operated from Balad as well. 3-58th AOB conducted its mission from Basra, while 412th ASB and the 12th CAB Headquarters were in Tallil, Iraq. Only the 412th ASB remained under the operational control of the 12th CAB Headquarters during the deployment. Every other deployed element was under the command of another military headquarters. 12th CAB did have operational control of several guard and reserve units, including the 1-130th ARB (National Guard from North Carolina), 2-285th AHB (National Guard from Arizona), C Company 3-238th GSAB (National Guard from New Hampshire), and B Company 5-159th GSAB (Reserve unit from Virginia).

As the bulk of the CAB returned to Germany in July of 2010, Charlie Company 1-214th Aviation deployed to South-West Afghanistan to provide Air Ambulance capability for U.S. Marines fighting there from July 2010 to August 2011, with one platoon remaining in the fight until November. During 214th's redeployment, one company from 3-159th ARB deployed separately to Tarin Kowt to augment forces already operating in Southern Afghanistan.

In February 2012, a sudden winter storm struck Montenegro, leaving hundreds of people stranded in the mountains of the Eastern European country. While the bulk of the Brigade was preparing for an upcoming deployment, 1-214th GSAB sent two UH-60 Blackhawk helicopters, with pilots, aircrews, and medical personnel to respond. While there, the crews worked with Montenegrin pilots and civilians and combined efforts with helicopters from Croatia, Slovenia, and Greece to deliver food and livestock feed, as well as to transport injured civilians to medical facilities there.

In May 2012, the CAB deployed five of its seven battalions to Afghanistan, while at the same time sending one attack battalion, 3-159th ARB, to Kuwait to support Operation Spartan Shield in the Persian Gulf. Only 1-214th remained in Germany. The aviation battalions were organized into similarly equipped task forces, each capable of providing the same mission and support to units operating in RC East, RC West and RC North. 3-58 AOB, known as TF Guardian, deployed to manage the airfield at Tarin Kowt in RC South. While the brigade headquarters redeployed in September as part of the drawdown of surge forces, the battalion task forces Storm, Gunslinger, Guardian, Ready and Pirate remained in Afghanistan providing direct support to units across the country. Task Force Pirate, an Air National Guard unit from Utah joined the Griffin Brigade for this deployment, providing seamless integration with their active duty counterparts in RC North. At the height of the deployment, 12 CAB had Soldiers and helicopter crews operating from more than 30 different locations.

In March 2013, for the first time since 2007, the entire 12 CAB returned to Germany where they continued to train and operate in support of EUCOM and AFRICOM contingency missions. G/52nd Aviation Company relocated to Wiesbaden from Manheim in 2013 and joined the 1-214th Aviation Regiment along with the VIP Company, Combat Aviation Detachment (CAD). 1-214th operated detachments in SHAPE, Belgium, Stuttgart, Germany, and a MEDEVAC company in Landstuhl Germany. By 2015, CAD, SHAPE, G/52nd along with the platoon in Stuttgart deactivated as the 1-214th began reorganizing and restructuring as a modern GSAB. The MEDEVAC Company, C Co. 1-214th relocated to Grafenwoehr and the CH-47s once part of 5-158th Aviation Regiment on Katterbach was re-designated as B Co. 1-214th GSAB.

In 2015, the 12 CAB began to draw down its formations. The 412th Aviation Support Battalion, 3-158th Assault Helicopter Battalion, 5-158th General Support Battalion, along with the 3-159th Attack Aviation Battalion was inactivated and restructured leaving the 1-214th GSAB as the only organic unit of the 12th Combat Aviation Brigade. After the Russian aggression in Crimea, an immediate halt to the drawn down led to the assignment of 1-3 AB to the 12 CAB.

The 12th Combat Aviation Brigade's headquarters, based in Bavaria's Ansbach Community, and its battalions reside at Katterbach, Grafenwoehr, and Wiesbaden Army Airfields. The 12th Combat Aviation Brigade currently consists of Headquarters and Headquarters Company, 12 CAB, 1-214th General Support Aviation Battalion, and 1-3 Attack Battalion.

Since its organization in 1965, the 12th Combat Aviation Brigade has served as a key member of the combined arms team, dedicated to the preservation of peace. The Brigade's motto, "Wings of Victory," continues to exemplify the standard by which the brigade conducts its missions in support of the United States of America.

Unit History courtesy of the 12th CAB Web-page (https://www.12cab.army.mil/)

3rd Battalion 158th Aviation Regiment "STORMRIDERS"
Assault Helicopter Battalion, 12th CAB, Germany

Battalion and Task Force patches

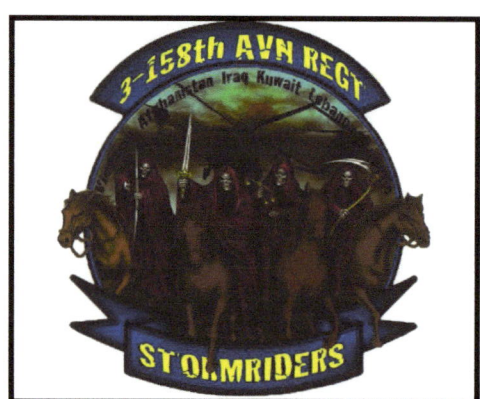
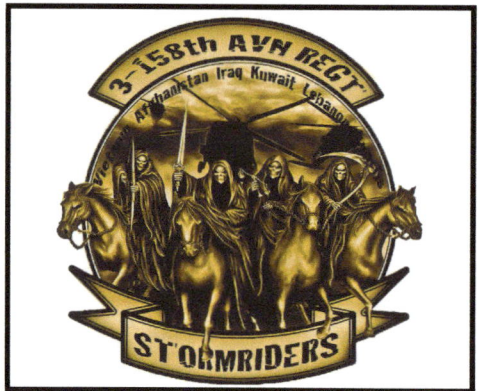

A Company 3-158 AVN "BLUE STARS"

  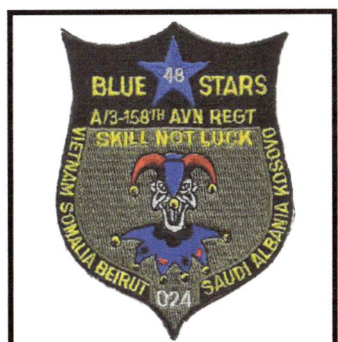 

B Company 3-158 AVN "WAR EAGLES"

| B Company continued... | C Company 3-158 AVN "WIZARDS" / "JOKERS" |

| HHC 3-158 AVN "NIGHT HAWKS" |

5th Battalion 158th Aviation Regiment
General Support Aviation Battalion, 12th CAB, Germany

Battalion patches

A Company 5-158 AVN "AMERICAN EXPRESS" / "FALCONS"

B Company 5-158 AVN "GARGOYLES" / "BIG WINDY"

B Company continued...

 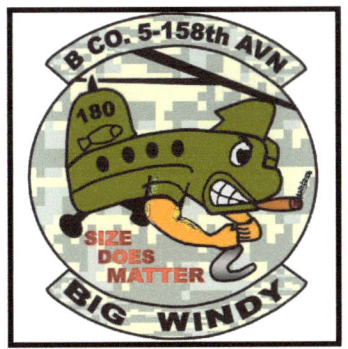   

C Company 5-158 AVN "RAPTORS" / "DUSTOFF"

D Company 5-158 AVN "DRAGONS"

HHC 5-158 AVN "FIGHTING KNIGHTS" / "HEADHUNTERS"

1st Battalion 214th Aviation Regiment

General Support Aviation Battalion, 12th CAB, Germany

Battalion patches

A Company 1-214 AVN "ACES"

B Company 1-214 AVN "BIG WINDY"

C Company 1-214 AVN "INTERNATIONAL DUSTOFF"

C Company continued...

D Company 1-214 AVN "SKYMASTERS" / "DEAD RABBITS"

E Company 1-214 AVN "BARONS"   HHC 1-214 AVN "DOGFIGHTERS"

16th Combat Aviation Brigade (16th CAB)

Joint Base Lewis McChord, Washington

History of the 16th CAB

The 16th Combat Aviation Group was formed in battle on 23 January 1968 under USARPAC General Order number 131. The unit was activated at Marble Mountain, Danang in the northern most part of south Vietnam. At the time of activation, the 16th Combat Aviation Group was formed from two battalions, the 14th Combat Aviation Battalion and the 212th Combat Support Aviation Battalion with a total combat force 3300 personnel.

Provisionally established in October 2005 at Fort Wainwright, Alaska Task Force 49 originally oversaw 4-123d Aviation Battalion, 1-52d Aviation Battalion, 68th Medical Company (Air Ambulance), and C-123d Aviation Maintenance Company. In February 2006, Task Force 49 was formally established, 4-123d Aviation Battalion was inactivated and 1-52d Aviation Battalion was reorganized into a General Support Aviation Battalion. 6-17th Cavalry Squadron and elements from the 209th Aviation Support Battalion were relocated from Wheeler Army Air Base, Hawaii to Fort Wainwright, Alaska in May 2006. While not part of the 16th CAB lineage, 6-17 CAV was under the command and control of 16th CAB from May 2006 to July 2011.

Beginning in July 2007, TF 49 had company elements continuously deployed for 31 consecutive months in support of Operation Iraqi Freedom. The first unit to deploy from Task Force 49 was the CH-47 based Task Force Dragon, composed primarily of B Company, 1-52d Aviation Battalion. Task Force Dragon supported two marine aircraft wings in Al Anbar, Iraq from July 2007 to August 2008. From November 2007 to December 2008, HHC, Task Force 49, deployed, and assumed command of the Multi-National Corps Iraq Aviation Brigade in support of Operation Iraqi Freedom and in July 2008, HHC Task Force 49 assumed command of the Multi-National Division-Center Aviation Brigade at Baghdad International Airport Iraq. 6th Squadron, 17th Cavalry deployed as Task Force Saber to Iraq in support of Operation Iraqi Freedom 08-09 with D Company, 123rd attached. The Squadron was awarded the Meritorious Unit Commendation for their performance in Northern Iraq from July 2008 to July 2009.

In November 2008, C/1-52 Med deployed for a year in support of OIF 08-10 and was assigned to Multi-National Division South, where they flew over 1000 combat MEDEVAC missions and saved countless lives. From February 2009 to February 2010, the GSABs Command Aviation Company, A/1-52, deployed to Iraq in support of MND-Center and MND-South. Throughout all of the brigades operational requirements in support of the Global War on Terror, C/123d AVIM deployed detachments and provided outstanding aircraft maintenance support.

On 16 October 2009, Headquarters and Headquarters Company Task Force 49 was re-designated as Headquarters and Headquarters Company 16th Combat Aviation Brigade, and activated at Fort Wainwright, Alaska becoming the Armys twelfth active duty Combat Aviation Brigade.

16th CABs first operational deployment was in August 2010 to provide Humanitarian Assistance to Pakistan. Task Force Denali, consisting of elements from 1-52 GSAB, C/123d AVIM and HHC/BDE, conducted a 100-day operation in response to Pakistans flood disaster.

In February 2011, 6-17 CAV and C/1-52 Medevac deployed to Iraq and Afghanistan respectively. 1-229 Attack Reconnaissance Battalion (AH-64), stationed at Fort Hood, Texas joined the 16th CAB in July 2010. 1-229th deployed to Iraq in support of Operation New Dawn in March 2011. In June, 2011, 1-52 deployed Team Denali, a CH-47 based unit, to Operation Enduring Freedom to support operations in southern Afghanistan. On 15 June, 2011, the 16th CAB cased the Brigades colors at Fort Wainwright, Alaska and moved the Headquarters and Headquarters Company to Joint Base Lewis McChord, Washington.

The colors were uncased at JBLM on 1 August, 2011, along with the activation of 2-158th Assault Helicopter Battalion (AHB) and 46th Aviation Support Battalion (ASB).

1st Battalion 52nd Aviation Regiment "FLYING DRAGONS"
General Support Aviation Battalion, 16th CAB, FT Richardson, AK

Battalion and Task Force patches

A Company 1-52 AVN "TOMAHAWKS"

B Company 1-52 AVN "SUGAR BEARS"

C Compnay 1-52 AVN "ARCTIC DUSTOFF"

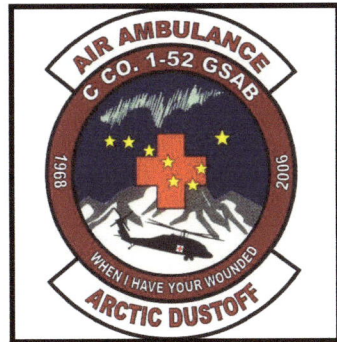 

D Company 1-52 AVN "OLD DUKES"

E Company 1-52 AVN "EAGLE SUPPORT"

F Company 1-52 AVN "ARCTIC FOX"

HHC 1-52 AVN "PIPELINE"

2nd Battalion 158th Aviation Regiment "WARHAWKS"

Assaut Helicopter Battalion, 16th CAB, Joint Base Lewis McChord, WA

Battalion patches

A Company 2-158 AVN "AXEMEN"

B Company 2-158 AVN "BIGFOOT"

C Company 2-158 AVN "SILVER SURFER" / "CRAZYHAWK"

D Company 2-158 AVN "DARK KNIGHT"	E Company 2-158 AVN "WAR EAGLE"

HHC 2-158 AVN "HONEY BADGERS" / "HURRICANES"

25th Combat Aviation Brigade (25th CAB) "WINGS of LIGHTNING"
25th Infantry Division. Wheeler Army Airfield, Hawaii

HISTORY of the 25th CAB

Activated at Schofield Barracks in 1957, the "Wings of Lightning" were originally designated as the 25th Aviation Company. The company earned two Meritorious Unit Commendations and two Valorous Unit Awards for its involvement in 12 Vietnam War campaigns.

In the early 1990s, several Wings of Lightning units participated in Operations Desert Shield and Storm and Hurricane Andrew relief efforts in Florida, then earned another Valorous Unit Award for involvement in Somalia.

CAB task forces also deployed in support of Operation Uphold Democracy in Haiti and Operation Joint Forge in Bosnia-Herzegovina.

When the Global War on Terrorism began, the CAB supported Operations Iraqi Freedom and Enduring Freedom V with tens of thousands of combat hours flown. 2009-10 saw aviation operations at COB Speicher in Tikrit, Iraq, until the brigade was needed in Kandahar, Afghanistan, during Operation Enduring Freedom 12-13.

Their mission as "Task Force Wings" earned them Aviation Unit of the Year (given by the Army Aviation Association) for many tactical developments and for being the first Army Medical Evacuation Helicopters to carry blood products on board. The 25th CAB earned three more Meritorious Unit Commendations for service in the Middle East between 2004-2009 and continues to serve the nation from its home in Hawaii.

2nd Battalion 25th Aviation Regiment "DIAMONDHEAD"

Assault Helicopter Battalion, 25th Infantry Division, Wheeler AAF, HI

Battalion and Task Force patches

A Company 2-25 AVN "BLACKJACK"

 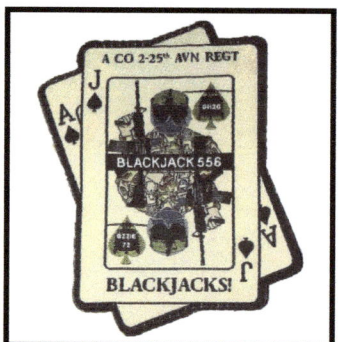   

B Company 2-25 AVN "KNIGHTHAWKS"

C Company 2-25 AVN "DARK HORSE" / "WOLF PACK"

D Company 2-25 AVN "CANNIBALS"

   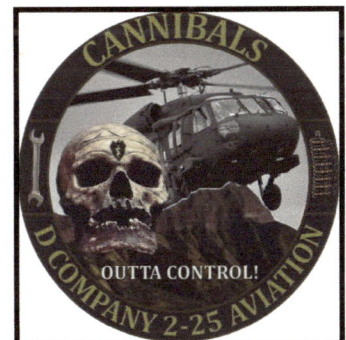

E Company 2-25 AVN "ROADRUNNERS"

HHC 2-25 AVN "TALONS"

3rd Battalion 25th Aviation Regiment "HAMMERHEADS"

General Support Aviation Battalion, 25th Infantry Division, WHeeler AAF, HI

Battalion and Task Force patches

A Company 3-25 AVN "STINGRAYS"

B Company 3-25 AVN "HILLCLIMBERS"

B Company continued...

C Company 3-25 AVN "LIGHTNING DUSTOFF"

D Company 3-25 AVN "TIGER SHARKS"

E Company 3-25 AVN "BARACUDAS"

HHC 3-25 AVN "MARLINS"

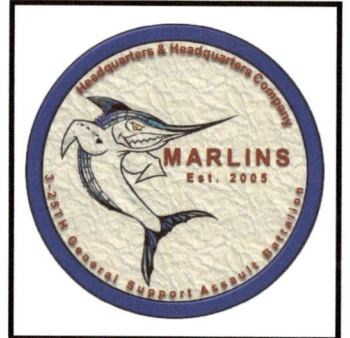

F Company 25th AVN "PATHFINDERS"   209th Aviation Support Battalion "LOBOS"

82nd Combat Aviation Brigade (82nd CAB) "PEGASUS"

82nd Airborne Division, Fort Bragg, North Carolina

On order, the 82nd Combat Aviation Brigade rapidly deploys in support of the Global Response Force to conduct decisive aviation operations worldwide to enable the ground force commander with air assault, air movement, attack, reconnaissance, and MEDEVAC capability.

The 82nd Combat Aviation Brigade tactical moniker "Pegasus" is a name drawn from the historic June 6th, 1944 Allied invasion of mainland Europe. Specifically, Pegasus Bridge was the single most important piece of key terrain whose control was critical to the protection of thousands of British and Canadian soldiers during their early morning assault on the beaches of Sword and Juno. British paratroopers were inserted on six gliders around midnight, the first Allied company sized unit to begin the D-Day invasion. These paratroopers used gliders to conduct air land insertions

The 82nd Combat Aviation Brigade prides itself as part of the 82nd Airborne Division.

Formed in 1957 as the 82nd Aviation Company and then later reorganized as the 82nd Aviation Battalion in 1960. The battalion became the first combat aviation battalion assigned to a division-sized unit in the U.S. Army. In 1987 the 82nd Aviation Battalion would again reorganized as the 82nd Aviation Brigade.

Since then, the "Wings of the Airborne" has always answered the nations call. Supporting operations in Vietnam, Desert Shield, Desert Storm, Dominican Republic, Panama, Grenade, the mountains of Afghanistan and the streets of Iraq.

Today's modern 82nd Combat Aviation Brigade (CAB) took shape in January 15, 2006. As the U.S. Army sought to better consolidate combat power through the Brigade Combat Team construct for its land forces, the aviation brigades underwent similar realignment to increase its capabilities. As a result of the reorganization of the 82nd Combat Aviation Brigade, the formation included: Headquarters and Headquarters Company (Gryphon), 1st Squadron, 17th Cavalry Regiment (Saber), 1st Attack Reconnaissance Battalion (Wolfpack), 2nd Assault Battalion (Corsair), 3rd General Support Aviation Battalion (Talon), and 122nd Aviation Support Battalion (Atlas).

2nd Battalion 82nd Aviation Regiment "CORSAIR"

Assault Helicopter Battalion, 82nd Airborne Division, Fort Bragg, NC

Battalion and Task Force patches

A Company 2-82 AVN "REDHAWKS"

B Company 2-82 AVN "CAVEMEN"

C Company 2-82 AVN "VIPERS"

D Company 2-82 AVN "DOG POUND"

E Company 2-82 AVN "LANCERS"

3rd Battalion 82nd Aviation Regiment "TALON"

General Support Aviation Battalion, 82nd Airborne Divsion, Fort Bragg, NC

Battalion and Task Force patches

A Company 3-82 AVN "MUSTANGS"

B Company 3-82 AVN "FLIPPERS"

B Company continued...

C Company 3-82 AVN "ALL AMERICAN DUSTOFF"

D Company 3-82 AVN "DARKHORSE"

HHC 3-82 AVN "GLADIATORS"

101st Combat Aviation Brigade (101st CAB) "WINGS of DESTINY"
101st Air Assualt Division, Fort Campbell, Kentuckey

History of the 101st CAB post 9/11

Beginning in January 2002, the brigade responded to the call of arms in support of Operation Enduring Freedom, fighting Taliban and al-Qaida forces in support of Task Force Rakkasan.

In February 2003, the brigade was alerted to deploy in support of Operation Iraqi Freedom. The brigade crossed the berm into Iraq on March 21, 2003, to launch deep attacks, as well as guard the V Corps' western flank. The brigade facilitated the liberation of three major cities and the coalition force's march on Baghdad.

After its redeployment from Operation Iraqi Freedom in spring 2004, to create a self-sustaining combat aviation brigade, the brigade transformed. Once this process was completed, the brigade again answered the nation's call in August 2005. The 101st Aviation Brigade began its second deployment in support of Operation Iraqi Freedom. Headquartered out of Contingency Operating Base Speicher in Tikrit, the brigade provided full-spectrum aviation support to the 101st Airborne Division (Air Assault), consisting of five brigade combat teams arrayed across 131,000 square kilometers of Band of Brothers' area of operation.

In December 2007, the 101st Combat Aviation Brigade, TF Destiny, deployed to Afghanistan in support of Operation Enduring Freedom. Headquartered in Bagram Airbase, the brigade task force provided full-spectrum aviation support to CJTF-82, CJTF-101, CJSOTF, and International Security and Assistance Forces (ISAF) arrayed across an area of responsibility the size of Texas.

In March 2010, the 101st Combat Aviation Brigade, TF Destiny, deployed to Afghanistan in support of Operation Enduring Freedom X. Headquartered in Kandahar Airbase, the brigade task force provided full-spectrum aviation support to CJTF-6 and CJTF-10, spread across Regional Command-South, an area of responsibility larger than Nebraska.

In June 2012, the 101st Combat Aviation Brigade, TF Destiny, deployed C Company, 6th Battalion, 101st CAB, Shadow Dustoff, a medevac unit; the rest of TF Destiny would deploy in August 2010. Task Force Destiny deployed as the Army's first full-spectrum combat aviation brigade after gaining a company of unmanned aerial vehicle operators. Headquartered in Bagram Airbase, the brigade task force provided full-spectrum aviation support to CJTF-1, CJTF-101, CJSOTF and ISAF arrayed across Regional Command-East.

After returning from Afghanistan in May of 2013, the brigade went into reset. During the reset, the brigade underwent a change of command in preparation for its next rendezvous with destiny.

In 2014, the brigade was tasked with conducting a flyover for Super Bowl XLVIII. On Feb. 2, 2014, three AH-64 Apache, three UH-60M Black Hawk and three CH-47 Chinook helicopters flew over MetLife Stadium at the conclusion of the national anthem.

In May 2014, the Wings of Destiny participated in exercise Golden Eagle. The exercise, which was a brigade-level air assault, was designed to update air-assault tactics techniques and procedures in The Gold Book, the manual which governs air-assault operations. In June of that year, the brigade participated in exercise Dark Eagle which further refined the lessons learned in Golden Eagle.

All throughout 2014, the brigade supported multiple rotations to the Joint Readiness Training Center in preparation for deployment.

In December 2014, four AH-64E Apache Guardian helicopters represented the 101st Airborne Division (Air Assault) at the Army-Navy Classic football game with a precision formation flyover.

101st CAB history continued...

In April 2015, the brigade deployed to Afghanistan to support Train Advise and Assist Command – East and South with aviation assets.

During 2015, 2nd Squadron, 17th Cavalry Regiment concluded the process of shutting down as the division's last OH-58D Kiowa Warrior unit. On March 31, 2015, 2-17th CAV conducted their final flight as a bittersweet sendoff to an aircraft that had come to define the squadron.

On July 17, 2015, 2-17th CAV inactivated, paving the way for a reactivation later.

On Sept. 10, 2015, 3rd Battalion, 101st CAB inactivated, and in the same ceremony activated as 2-17th CAV, updating the squadron's firepower from the OH-58D Kiowa Warrior to AH-64 Apache helicopter.

Task Force Destiny redeployed in late 2015.

The Destiny Brigade cased the colors for one of the three remaining Pathfinder companies in the U.S. Army arsenal during an inactivation ceremony for Fox Co. (Pathfinders) 5-101 "Eagle Assault" Aug. 2, 2016.

In August 2017 2nd Squadron, 17th Cavalry Regiment deployed to Southwest Asia in support of Operation Spartan Shield.

The 101st CAB cased its colors in May 2018 for its fifth deployment to Afghanistan as part of a regular rotation of forces to support Operation Freedom's Sentinel.

The 101st Combat Aviation Brigade is continually at the forefront of Army aviation. Honor, duty and innovation are the hallmarks of the Soldiers who continue the proud tradition of the Wings of Destiny. (CAB history via 101st CAB homepage: https://home.army.mil/campbell/index.php/units/history)

A CH-47F from B CO 6-101 AVN 101st AA Division (photo by Author)

4th Battalion 101st Aviation Regiment "WINGS of the EAGLE"

Assault Helicopter Battalion, 101st Air Assault Division, FT Campbell, KY

Battalion and Task Force patches

Author's Note: 4-101 AVN was assigned to the 159th CAB at the beginning of the GWOT. For the sake of simplicity the patches of 4th and 7th Battalions which were assigned to the 159th CAB until 2015 will be posted under the banner of the 101st CAB.

A Company 4-101 AVN "COMMANCHEROS"

B Company 4-101 AVN "KINGSMEN"

C Company 4-101 AVN "BLACKWIDOWS"

D Company 4-101 AVN "DESPERADOS"

HHC 4-101 AVN "HAWKS"

5th Battalion 101st Aviation Regiment "EAGLE ASSAULT"

Assault Helicopter Battalion, 101st Air Assault Division, FT Campbell, KY

Battalion and Task Force patches

A Company 5-101 AVN "PHOENIX"

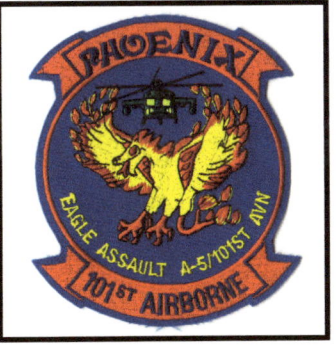    

B Company 5-101 AVN "LANCER"

C Company 5-101 AVN "PHANTOMS"

| D Company 5-101 AVN "GHOSTRIDERS" | E Company 5-101 AVN "RENEGADES" |

| HHC 5-101 AVN "RAIDERS" |

6th Battalion 101st Aviation Regiment "SHADOW of the EAGLE"
General Support Aviation Battalion, 101st Air Assault Division, FT Campbell, KY

Battalion and Task Force patches

A Company 6-101 AVN "WARLORDS"

B Company 6-101 AVN "WARLORDS" / "PACHYDERMS"

  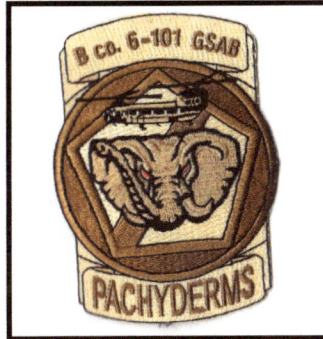  

B Company continued...

C Company 6-101 AVN "RUDE DOGS" / "SHADOW DUSTOFF"

   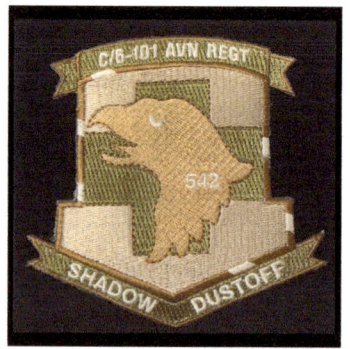

C Company continued...

D Company 6-101 AVN "WITCHDOCTORS"

F Company 6-101 AVN "SKYMASTERS"

HHC 6-101 AVN "IRON EAGLES"

7th Battalion 101st Aviation Regiment "EAGLE LIFT"

General Support Aviation Battalion, 101st Air Assault Division, Fort Campbell, KY

Battalion and Task Force patches

Author's Note: *7-101 AVN was assigned to the 159th CAB at the beginning of the GWOT. For the sake of simplicity the patches of 4th and 7th Battalions which were assigned to the 159th CAB until 2015 will be posted under the banner of the 101st CAB.*

A Company 7-101 AVN "PREDATORS" / "RUDE DOGS"

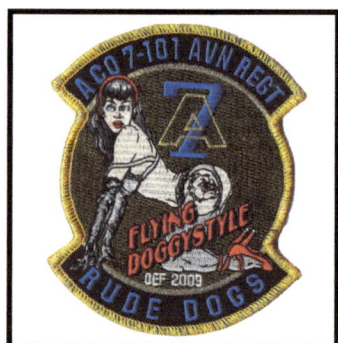

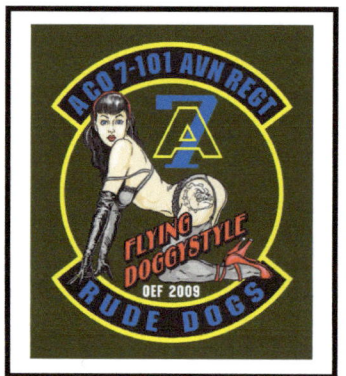

B Company 7-101 AVN "VARSITY"

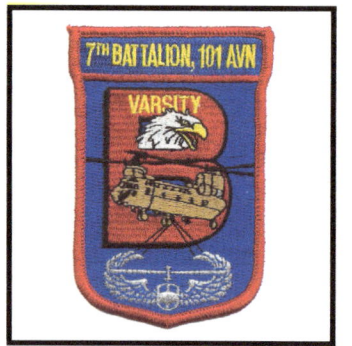

C Company 7-101 AVN "OUTLAWS" / "EAGLE DUSTOFF"

  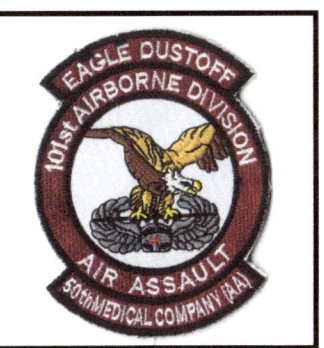  

D Company 7-101 AVN "DRAGONS"

G Company 7-101 AVN "REAPERS"

HHC 7-101 AVN "HOOKERS" / FIGHTING GRIFFINS"

159th Combat Aviation Brigade (159th CAB)

101st Air Assault Division, Fort Campbell, KY

159th Aviation Regiment DUI

Task Force Thunder 159th CAB (2014)

Task Force Attack 159th CAB (2009)

159th CAB Helmet patch

History of the 159th CAB

159th Combat Aviation Brigade History
The 159th Combat Aviation Brigade (CAB) formerly supported the 101st Airborne Division (Air Assault), and was stationed at Fort Campbell, Kentucky. While active, 159th CAB made the 101st Airborne Division the only US Army Division with two organic aviation brigades, and currently the 101st CAB is the only CAB supporting the unit at Fort Campbell. The 159th CAB was inactivated on 15 May 2015.

The lineage of the 159th Aviation Brigade is separate from that of the Vietnam-era 159th Aviation Battalion and the later 159th Aviation Regiment
The 159th Aviation Battalion (Assault Helicopter) was a Vietnam War-era heavy lift helicopter unit formed on 1 July 1968 from the assets of the 308th Aviation Battalion (Combat). The spiritual ancestor (separate lineage) to the 159th CAB was organized as the medium and heavy lift Assault Helicopter Battalion of the 101st Airborne Division, and composed of three Boeing CH-47 Chinook companies (Pachyderms - A Company; Varsity - B Company; Playtex - C Co) and 1 Sikorsky CH-54 Tarhe company (Hurricanes). In the modern formation, only "Varsity" Company remained as Company B, 7th Battalion, 101st Aviation Regiment, 159th CAB.

From January 1969 through February 1972, the battalion provided lift support to the 101st Airborne. The unit conducted airmobile artillery raids, troop movements, flare drops, fire-base insertions and extractions, IFR airdrops, and flight support and aircraft recovery missions. The 159th Aviation Battalion received the Valorous Unit Award for services in the Republic of Vietnam, 1 January 1970 through May 1971. In February 1972, the 159th Aviation Battalion returned to Fort Campbell, Kentucky as the only CH-47 Chinook battalion in the United States Army.

In November 1987, the 159th Aviation Battalion headquarters was inactivated at Fort Campbell and the 159th Aviation Regiment was activated under the new U.S. Army regimental system at Fort Bragg, North Carolina. Later, the unit would be redesignated as 4th Battalion, 159th Aviation Regiment and was activated at Kitzingen, Germany, and then relocated to Giebelstadt, Germany. From this point on, the 159th Aviation Regiment would have no further affiliation with either Fort Campbell, the 101st Airborne, or the 159th Aviation Brigade - the 159th Aviation Regiment continues to exist as a separate unit affiliated with 12th Aviation Brigade.

101st Aviation Regiment
Meanwhile, the same 1987 reorganization that removed the 159th Aviation Battalion lineage left nine active aviation battalions which had existed beneath it at Fort Campbell. As such, these units were assigned lineage to the 101st Aviation Regiment, and initially reformed under the headquarters of the 101st Aviation Brigade.
As originally formed, Sikorsky UH-60 Black Hawks were in the 4th, 5th and 9th Battalions, 101st Aviation; Bell UH-1 Iroquois were in the 6th Battalion, 101st Aviation; CH-47D Chinooks were in the 7th Battalion, 101st Aviation; and Boeing AH-64 Apache were in 1st, 2nd and 3rd Battalion, 101st Aviation. Aviation support was provided by 8th Battalion, 101st Aviation Regiment.

Serious flaws with this arrangement would become apparent during the First Gulf War, as the resulting nine Battalion unit was the size of some regiments yet lacked an adequately sized staff element, headquarters, or officer rank to control such a large unit over a wide area. As a result, the 101st Airborne headquarters considered breaking the 101st Aviation Brigade in half and establishing a second headquarters.

The 159th Aviation Brigade
On 9 October 1997, the largest aviation brigade in the Army split nine battalions into two brigades, the 101st Aviation Brigade (Attack) and the 159th Aviation Brigade (Assault). Between 1997 and 2001, the Brigade deployed units to Bosnia, Kosovo, Trinidad and Tobago, and Central America.

History of the 159th CAB continued...

Post 9/11
2002 Afghanistan deployment
Following 9/11, elements of the 4-101st (Blackhawk), and 7-101st (Chinook) Aviation Battalions, 159th Aviation Brigade deployed to Afghanistan in support of Operation Enduring Freedom. Deploying 29 January 2002 for OEF, 159th elements prepared and strategically deployed 5 UH-60L Blackhawk aircraft and 6.5 aircrews to Kandahar, Afghanistan. 159th Brigade also deployed 8 UH-60L Blackhawk and 13 CH-47 Chinook aircraft to Bagram.

The unit deployed another 5 UH-60L aircraft to Bagram Air Force Base, Afghanistan on 3 May 2002. In September 2002, two elements of A Company, 4-101st Aviation Regiment redeployed from Afghanistan where they supported OEF in the fight against the Taliban.

On 20 November 2014, the U.S. Army announced that the 159th CAB would be inactivated in 2015. As part of the restructuring, the Army will retain the 159th CAB's Apache battalion, the 3d Battalion (Attack/Reconnaissance), 101st Aviation Regiment, and reassign it to the 101st CAB. The majority of 159th CAB Soldiers would be sent elsewhere

OEF DEPLOYMENTS: 4
OIF DEPLOYMENTS: 1

501st Combat Aviation Brigade (501st CAB) "IRON EAGLES"

1st Armored Division, Fort Bliss, Texas

History of the 501st CAB (Also known as 1AD CAB)

The Combat Aviation Brigade, 1st Armored Division "Iron Eagles" was first constituted April 16, 1986, at Ansbach, Germany. Three and a half years later, the Iron Eagles deployed to Southwest Asia in support of Operations Desert Shield and Desert Storm. Upon redeployment, the unit relocated in September 1991 to Erlensee, Germany.

In December 1995, the Iron Eagles deployed to Operation Joint Endeavor to Bosnia-Herzegovina as part of a multinational peace implementation force. The brigade would again support peace-keeping efforts in the Balkans from June 2000 to June 2001 by deploying two task forces. From April 2003 to July 2004, the Combat Aviation Brigade deployed to Iraq in support of Operation Iraqi Freedom, where they played a significant role in the security and stabilization of Iraq and its people. Then on July 7, 2006, the unit cased its colors and was inactivated.

September 20, 2011, marked a historic moment for the Combat Aviation Brigade. After being separated from 1st Armored Division for five years, the Iron Eagles of the Division's Combat Aviation Brigade and the Iron Soldiers of the 1st Armored Division reunited during the brigade's activation ceremony at Fort Bliss, Texas. With this final brigade's arrival, the 1st Armored Division completed the Army's largest Base Realignment and Closure move, and the CAB began its integration of more than 1,200 families into both the Fort Bliss and El Paso communities. Following re-stationing of the CAB to Fort Bliss, the Iron Eagles participated in numerous training exercises, to include the installation-wide training event known as Iron Focus, three Network Integration Exercises, and the three month-long Culminating Training Event that simultaneously deployed the entire brigade to five different locations throughout the southern United States.

In December 2012, and just 15 months after activation and re-stationing, the CAB self-deployed the 4-501 Attack Reconnaissance Battalion to Operation Spartan Shield. The CAB then deployed Task Force 1-501 ARB, TF 3-501 AHB, and elements of 2-501 GSAB and 127th ASB to Afghanistan in support of Operation Enduring Freedom in February 2013.

In January 2019, the 1AD CAB, as TF Iron Eagle, deployed to Afghanistan in support of Operation Freedom's Sentinel. As the largest task force within the CJOA-A, TF Iron Eagle flew 58,000 combat hours conducting aerial reconnaissance, attack and lift operations in support of Resolute Support partners and Afghan forces. The deployment culminated in the completion of about 1,200 deliberate and hasty operations, movement of over 93,000 personnel and a multitude of improvements to sustainment operations, setting the conditions for ongoing aviation operations within the CJOA-A.

2nd Battalion 501st Aviation Regiment "DESERT KNIGHTS"

General Support Aviation Battalion, 1st Armored Division, FT Bliss, TX

Battalion and Task Force patches

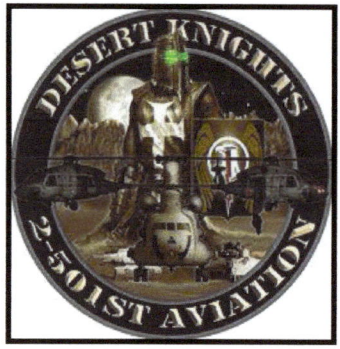

A Company 2-501 AVN "BLACK CATS"

B Company 2-501 "BLACK KNIGHTS"

C Company 2-501 AVN "GHOSTRIDERS" / "LONE STAR DUSTOFF"

| D Company 2-501 AVN "DRAGONSLAYERS" | E Company 2-501 AVN "TEMPLARS" |

| F Company 2-501 AVN "KNIGHT WATCHERS" |

3rd Battalion 501st Aviation Regiment "APOCALYPSE"

Assault Helicopter Battalion, 1st Armored Division, FT Bliss, TX

Battalion and Task Force patches

Battalion patches continued...

A Company 3-501 AVN "ARCHANGELS"

B Company 3-501 AVN "BEAST ASSAULT"

B Company continued...

C Company 3-501 AVN "CHAOS"

D Company 3-501 AVN "DEMONS"

E Company 3-501 AVN "ENFORCERS"   HHC 3-501 AVN "HELL HOUNDS"

Miscellaneous Units (AKA Everything Else)

1st Battalion 212th Aviation Regiment, Fort Rucker, Alabama

| A Company 1-212 AVN | C Company 1-212 AVN | E Company 1-212 AVN |

F Company 1-212 AVN

Flight School Class patches

Flight School patches continued...

12th Aviation Battalion, Military District of Washington

Battalion patches

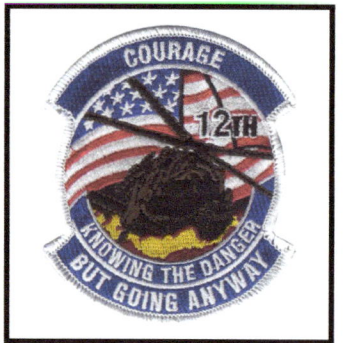
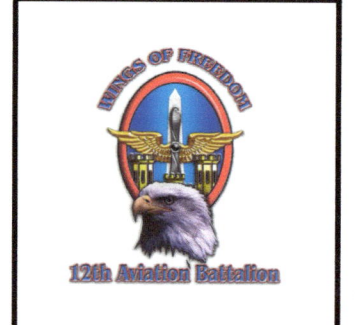

A Company 12th AVN BN "VIPERS"			B Company 12th AVN BN "BLACK SHEEP"	

C Company 12th AVN BN "CON AIR"		D Company 12th AVN BN	HHC 12th AVN BN "BLACK KNiGHTS"

78th Aviation Battalion, Camp Zama, Japan

Battaion patches

| USA Jet Detatchment, Japan | A Company 78th AVN BN "RAVENS" |

1-228th AVN Battalion, Soto Cano Airbase, Honduras

| C Company 1-228 AVN   "WITCH DOCTORS" |

| D Company 1-228 AVN | HHC 1-228 AVN "PHANTOMS" |

2916th AVN Battalion, National Training Center, Fort Irwin, CA

A Company 2916th AVN BN "DESERT HAWKS"

B Company 2916th AVN BN "OPFOR"

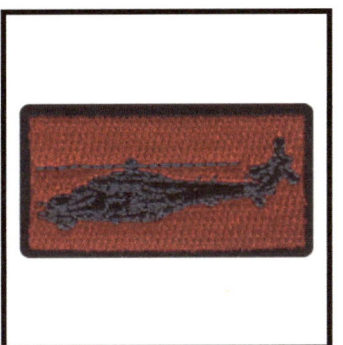

C Company 2916th AVN BN "DESERT DUSTOFF"

NTC Aviation Observer/Controllers "EAGLE TEAM"

CONTRIBUTORS

There is no way that this book could have ever been made without the help of a lot of other people. Below is a list of some of the many folks who helped in getting me images or actual patches to be included in this project. Unfortunately some of these folks are no longer with us. This hobby will be poorer in their absence but we are all richer for having known them. Everything good in this book is because of these fine folks.

THANK YOU!

Aeroemblem, Keith Alan, Apache Warrior Foundation, Emil Balusek (RIP), David Barber, Paul Belobrajdic, Joe Belsha, Keith Benner, Steve Boras, Perry Bowden, Jack Brink, Steve Bull, Brian Carbone, Clint Chamberland, Ashlie Christian, Jeff Crownover, Dan Cruz, Tim Dolifka (RIP), Kevin Dishner, Chris Dixon, Al Dupre, Rod Dwyer, Daniel Flores, Bill Fox, Carl Fox, Jake Gaston, Nick Hatchel, Glen Hees, Mark Hough, Britton Howell, Aaron Joe, Micah Johnson, Eric Jurarez, Christopher Koth, Aaron Krupa, Billy L LeJeune, Keith Lindsey, Jef Litvin, CW4 Matt Lourey (RIP), Ryan Madar, Angelica Maria, Jim McLean, Herbert McTacops, Fox Mike, Russ Mixon, Samuel Mo, CV Nance, Ryan Nelson, Matthew Norbury, Robert Reardon, Alec Record, Steve Reynolds, Lea A. Rhinehart, Jason Richards, Angelo Rickert, Jennifer Gruber Roach, Tom Rude, Alan Sanders, Steven Sandoval, Rocky Sudduth, Brian Serna, Mark Shaw, Carl Smith, Dustin Smith, Keith Snyder, Jay Son, Shaun Steines, Tad Stuart, Shaun Thurman, Jeffrey Trombly, US Company, Pascal Vermeersch, Seth Vieux, Andy Wilson, and Alan Woods

"HEY, WHERE"S MY PATCH?"

If your patch or your unit was inadvertently left out of this book or we got something wrong, we apologize. We want to make this book as accurate as possible, so if you would be nice enough to send an image and a short explanation of the patch to dngrpig@ gmail.com, we will make sure it's included in future editions and your name will be added to the list of contributors.

THANK YOU FOR YOUR COMMITMENT TO THE HISTORY OF ARMY AVIATION!

.

www.ingramcontent.com/pod-product-compliance
Lightning Source LLC
Chambersburg PA
CBHW041325290426

44109CB00004B/122